T. Gardner

THE MYTH OF A WOMAN'S FIST

Books by Ann Darr

THE MYTH OF A WOMAN'S FIST
ST ANN'S GUT

THE MYTH
of a
WOMAN'S FIST
by Ann Darr

William Morrow & Company, Inc.
New York 1973

Copyright © 1961, 1962, 1965, 1969, 1971, 1972, 1973 by Ann Darr

All rights reserved. No part of this book may be reproduced or utilized in any form or by any means, electronic or mechanical, including photocopying, recording or by any information storage and retrieval system, without permission in writing from the Publisher. Inquiries should be addressed to William Morrow and Company, Inc., 105 Madison Ave., New York, N.Y. 10016.
Design by Helen Roberts
Printed in the United States of America.

1 2 3 4 5 77 76 75 74 73

Library of Congress Cataloging in Publication Data

Darr, Ann.
    The myth of a woman's fist.

    Poems.
    I. Title.
PS3554.A73M9   811'.5'4   73-11412
ISBN 0-688-00215-3
ISBN 0-688-05215-0 (pbk.)

for Elizabeth, Deborah and Shannon

Acknowledgments

Some of these poems have been published in the following journals: *Antaeus, Buffalo Stamps, Charles Street Journal, Choice, Contempora, December, Dryad, Mill Mountain Review, The New York Times, New Mexico Quarterly, Noise, Northeast, Phoebe, Salt Lick, Vanderbilt Poetry Review, Voyages, Woodwind.*

Contents

"Send a Biographical Note . . ."	1
Down/Beat	2
Styx	3
No Right	4
The Myth of a Woman's Fist	5
Brother	7
—ESS	8
The Stone Under the Skin	9
Unlikely Reply to a Letter from Bucks County, Pennsylvania	14
Memo from 1972	15
High Dark	16
Hand	20
Evolution	21
Visit to an Empty House	22
Freeze	23
For a Giacometti	25
At What Point	27
"Hit It with the Baby"	28
Poem Found in an Old George Garrett Footprint	29
Signals for Anti-Hijacking	31
Ruminations After Saying No to Giving a College Graduation Address	33
Push	34
The Bagley Iowa Poem	35
Orders	39
Separation Blues in E^b	40
Place Counts	41
In Retrospect	42
Conjure Blues	43

Nightshade Family	44
A Measure of Hate	45
Every Now and Then at Night	47
Lines Written While Landing at La Guardia	48
Gussie Sends Quick Letter	50
The Witch of Calmés	51
Looking for Origins	52
Country Tract	53
Homing	54
Distance	55
The Case of the Red Dotted Swiss	56
Death Watch	57
The Trip	59
Two Men in Tractor Time	60
To a Father Stewing About His Sons	62
Bone-China Woman	63
History Has Struck Her Repeat Button	64
Note to the Young Girl Who Has Just Won a Poetry Prize	65
The Animal Standing There	67
Late Last Night with Southern Comfort	69
November Park	70
To Write	71
Until Cremation Is Required	72
The Formula	73
Yorick Rides Again	74
They Asked Me What I Wanted	82

The mind is a violence from within protecting us from a violence without. It is the imagination pressing back against the pressure of reality. It seems, in the last analysis, to have something to do with our self-preservation: and that, no doubt, is why the expression of it, the sound of its words, helps us to live our lives.
—WALLACE STEVENS

"Send a Biographical Note..."

I have published poems in the Potomac
    River, on Grand Teton Mountain,
        and on the beach at Piraeus.

They were all written
    in an old Indian dialect
        unknown even to Ishi.

I make instant translations
    constantly.
        With everyone.

I alternate between telling
    everything I know, and being
        afraid to speak.

I am made up of everyone
    I have ever encountered.
I am still everywhere
    I have ever been.

I know the wilderness
    is necessary. I do not want
        to live there.

I feel the planet turn away from me.
I am traveling without laughter.

Down/Beat

I rhymed my ears and braided my arms
for a laughing thread to tie
on my thumb. Psoriasis. I have come
down with galloping psoriasis,
have need of crutches for my tongue,
I am splinted all the way from
cerebrum to candelabra.

       I limp home licking my wounded
poems. For rhyme I strike
       two matches.

       I have been down before, down
on my luck, down on my knees,
down to the bottom of the well
I doused with my own cut apple staff.
       I have been cut down.

       I have chased words across
continents. Into layers of cumulo-
nimbus. I open a great round mouth.
No sound comes out. From the bottom
of the well comes a sodden sobbing.

How shall I tell you that the demons are
real? that a poem is really a scale
from a monstrous hide. RUN.

Styx

Come on get in, he says, but
I am busy dismantling the dock.

He switches boats to a tri-
maran, heels on one glider,

looking for all the world like
a dancer in mid-dance. I

am breathing heavily, tasting salt.
He tacks and heads for shore,

I back away. I must leave
the river's bank, the lake's

shore, the sea's edge, I must
retreat to root country.

But the moving surfaces call.
I dream of water, water.

I am the last of my family.

No Right

What can I do to feel close to you?
Put on something belonging to you—
your long blue cape embroidered
        with blood.

I am flying into the sunset
too many times. I am speeding
west and on this day I have seen
        seven sunsets.

The sun is always going down,
we are rounding the corner speeding,
there is an aura of color—
        splintering glass.

Suicide is for the upper class.
Down here there are only accidents,
a hunting episode, the speeding car,
        the startled ditch.

But where are the children of the oven
breathers? Child of the slashed wrists
where are you—of the heavy accelerator
foot—child of the barbed wire face—
        here in this ditch mama here.

The Myth of a Woman's Fist

The myth about
a woman's fist,
(putting the thumb
inside), still
makes me flex
my hand to check,
though I have known
since it was first
told to me
as solemn truth
it was a lie.

Told to me
by the man who
sent me solo
in a plane.
I had to believe
everything he
told me.
I believed
some myth about
if any part
were lie,
it all was.
So man couldn't
fly, nor woman either,
nor any bird-form
outside of birds themselves

could rise and soar
and glide.

What I learned
on that first flight
alone
was that I sing
when I'm afraid.

Perhaps it is myth
that music tries to match
the music of the spheres,
or that the impetus is praise.
Maybe all the music of the world
is to ward off fear.

Brother

Brother is such a solid word
to splinter on the rocks.
I never planned it any way at all.
Drop your rabbit right down
here, and hollow chocolate
shattered on the floor.
I remained his enemy.
Blood is thicker than water,
but swimming in it this way,
side-stroke, is to arrive
on the far side of forgiveness
with nothing in my arms
        but air.

–ESS

I look too much like
that suicidess
to be happy in the dark.

Waves of peanut butter
surge over me, pilotess,
    gardeneress
    danceress,

canoess, fisheress,
    a trademark-
    ess, a cookess,
    smokeress.

Robert Graves (I read
    your essay *ess*)
    forgivess
    me ess.

The Stone Under the Skin

     1.

The way the wind comes
through these cracks
at the window sills
should have warned us.
We had meant to shut out
cold, meant to hold
fire serenely in a room
where rafters bent
in a way to warm our eyes,
echoing mountains.
     I came to the tall pines
     ready to grow straight.
     I was not prepared
     for the warping wind.
Bitter words warp
our best intentions,
shriek through our private sills,
chilling the family tree.
These rafters
bow down across
strafed chests,
make the breathing hard.
This is a climate

we had not bargained for.
Frost forms on familiar
tongues, nostrils spread.
We are an endangered species.

      2.

When the Chinese Acrobats twirled
their plates on the ends of wands,
I applauded wildly and found
a new stone in the palm of my hand.

The Chinese Magician brought forth
a fish on the end of his line
extended over the audience.
I found a stone fish in my palm.

One Bicycle Rider gathered
twenty riders on her round,
I found a stone wheel
in the middle of my hand.

      3.

I thought I had reconciled
my angle of mercy.

Haven't I killed off
all my enemies, in my head?
Warped them into strange tree-
trunks they can't climb down?
Obviously not. Instead,
I have back-mastered
an inglorious statue,
turning myself to
stone.

If humor really cured
my doting head,
I could have laughed myself
into obscurity. instead
I have stoned myself
into obliquity.
I am afraid of what
lies ahead.

4.

We cut a hole in the ice
and fished for reasons.
Winter sat tight on
our shoulder blades.

the air filled with
hot answers.

I must find
the match to light the fire.
this smouldering under snow
will only come to water.

the flood took place
too long ago. It iced
into this way of life.
Somewhere there is an owl

flying.

If I must turn to
stone, first I must find
the position to be
stoned to.

5.

damn winter.
I lurch through snow
that hasn't fallen.

cold ache
of residual
aftermath
of heat.
the argument
has burned
through all
my defenses
left
a deep pain
burning
out of sight.
winter
should bring
rest
but this
climate
has axed
the sleep
of forebears,
and they bleed
across the snow
that hasn't
fallen.

Unlikely Reply to a Letter from Bucks County, Pennsylvania

for Eric Knight, the Flying Yorkshireman

The wind is from the east holding
the flag horizontally over
the White House canceled boldly
by four black lines and a firm
round post-mark of PLEASANT VALLEY
looking like a new-minted dollar.

I receive a time jolt through
this unopened envelope as if Eric
were still marching somewhere
in Princess Pat's Regiment
instead of crashing with Leslie
Howard in a different war.

                As if
your translucent white silk calf
had just arrived on your Pennsylvania hill
and we are still burying it
in a shallow grave, still digging it
up, after the Vet said "Sure it's dead?"
as he went elbow deep for the lost
placenta. "Bessie's still shitten
soapsuds" you said hours later
when the plate glass mirror fell
off the wall and bounced on
the overstuffed chair.

                    And still in summer
that changing-cell philosophy falls apart
when the ivy twists over my skin in angry
red tendrils beginning with undressing shyly
beyond the tree, in the poison patch.

Memo from 1972

I would like to tell you that
the wind sock is on the other foot
(the second sock is always hard to knit)

but that would be lying.
I would like to say I have grown golden
feathers over the old scar, that the blue

windmill still turns, flowering above
the mulberry tree. But that isn't true.

Nothing covers the scar but words. The windmill was always two inches high, and the feathers
have grown damp and smell of damp feathers.

High Dark

The camera that takes the pictures after the fact
can focus on any black night
over Sweetwater and find me still
circling, still wheeling for the final turn,
traveling at a breakneck speed,
hunting the level invisible earth,
still unable
to land.

On that first night solo flying
swallowed by the night,
trying to cough myself up, I must trust
all night flyers to steer clear of me . . .
bats be my friends, do your counting
out of my rectangle, owls, lay over on
some branch and hoot from there,
I cannot feather my wings. I
cannot find the field.

    I must not keep on at high speed
into the black air, am I going up or down,
are the stars above me or is it my city,
Sweetwater, sweet water, bring me down.
I cannot keep speeding through air.
I dare *not* keep speeding through air,
there is only one place I can arrive.
On earth. No place else will accept me

with active eyes and ears.
I have become two beings, one skin
standing a space away from the other
like a picture frame. Hurtling through air
I must make decisions that stand still
so I can perform them. Or die.
      Die? Not yet. Wipe out the pictures
of my life flashing before my eyes. That is cliché
and doesn't really happen. I am obverse enough to
have it begin. Reel one. Roll one: I am being
dangled upside down on the roof of the house
I know I was born in . . . over a balcony
with a railing of tooled poles . . . looking like
New Orleans, but it stood at the end of
the only street in town and standing on
that balcony you could watch the crops go by
year after year—cornfields end on end to an horizon
that ended because the earth curved.
      My horizon is where the earth
is curving, joined in black velvet
with the space that is curving, my plane
track is curving and I must not curve, I must
set this plane down on a straight runway. on
a level plain. before the gas gives out.

Four times now I have maneuvered into place
made the proper angle to bring me nose-straight

into the flight pattern . . . four times the rows of
yellow pearls have grown in size too soon.
and I have pulled up hard and flown on, shaken
by all my errors. I have never wanted
jewels much. I have never wanted jewels so much
in all my life. o lights. o stars.
o bats. winged creatures of the night . . .
o fraud. I have no right to join you.
I donate my wings to you—I would strip
them off if I could and give you my wings
for a house. Here I give you my engine,
my lights, my instruments, my radio, my
helmet, here—have my parachute.
I have no chance to use it.
If I opened the hatch now and stepped out,
I would discover only after I started falling
which way was down. Throw everything
overboard. Deep-six it all. Government
issue be-damned. But turn another corner,
bring the yellow pearls in sight. my god,
don't lose the field. Let gravity work.
Keep my fellow flyers away from me. Stop
magnetism. Sweat the parachute wet,
if you have to, but don't lose the field.

    One last attempt. Last?
I will keep on trying until

we are flying only by riding the wind—
except this is no glider and will plummet—
stop. I have stopped the newsreel. I
have stopped time. I am diving at great speed
into the black earth, pull up, pull, make the angle
right, let down the landing gear, now now! without
the wheels I will nose over—whack the landing gear
release—in place, we are moving
for our lives, this plane and me, flaps down, level,
not on one wheel—vertigo abhors a vacuum—level—there!
there is the touch, there is that moment in time when I am
    touching
the earth again, the wheels are part of my belly, I am hugging
    the earth
I am down.

But cover both your ears, and the sound you hear
is my plane still flying lost, still circling the dark,
and I frantic, knowing only if I do not panic can I reach home,
knowing I will always be circling, lost in the dark, traveling
at high speed, knowing it for what it is.

Hand

I tried to learn
to read palms
    but
all I know is
when the lines
glisten with sweat
    like this,
something is happening
   somewhere else.

Evolution

I am the fish. I speak to you
from the ocean.
You have called me star.
You have designated me a holy symbol.
As your crown of thorns, I shall eat
                you up.
I would have given you another
hundred thousand years, but
your home-made birds have changed
                all that.
You have carried me by jet
to your most prosperous landscape.
I speak to you from the land.
I move north across Florida
eating my own kind.
Eating everything in my path.
I am the fish. I am holy. I am
                hungry.

Visit to an Empty House

Walked on your porch today,
threaded my way
through the ancient cardboard boxes.
Bored hiss of an old analytic hour
seeped over the ledge
like canning gone sour.

    When you began to call my man
        by your man's name,
  (your man lost so many years before)
        then I began to focus
    not on me but you, the mad old
        Madam of Sick Street.

You were in love
with the sound of your voice
and the hair
on the back of your hand.

Freeze

January froze solid. Stopped all talk
about a January thaw. And the Saturday
with strawberries came much later
in the century.
        forgive me, I have not answered
        your letter, I have lost your
        address, your face.
So there we sat on the edge of that
frozen river, while old Ma Muse
turned us into white marble with
her little hatchet. (I cannot
tell a lie. I did it with. There are no
lies. It is all truth. If you imagine it,
saith the holies, that's it,
brother.) I skated all over
that river as if I'd grown the skates
especially for the purpose. I felt
this funny itching in the bottoms
of my feet. (I know too much about
insects. Don't think I don't remember
all those forays with the matches burning
every last ring of springs under those old
mattresses) but that wasn't it. This
was silver and fine and slick and sharp
and coming out the bottoms of my feet
and I am knowing what miracles are about
and this is all a lot of lies. I didn't

grow skates at all. Hands put those skates
on me. But this part's true. I couldn't
skate before and I can't skate since, but
that day I was Mercury across the ice.
(Thin ice is too easy. Thick ice
is too slick.)
        I cannot find the letters.
        I believe I may have
        published them.
January-Stanuary Kubrickity, none of your
monster shows have been more unreal.
We are still on the shore of that frozen
river. The light is pallid pinks and blues.
dear god, let me freeze to death, I am afraid
of drowning.
        Do not send letters. Send
        the hands that laced the skates.

For a Giacometti

Alberto
could put
all his
little people,
heads pin-pointed,
bodies wizened up,
in a box
and drive out of Paris
with the box
on the back
of his bicycle,
a day ahead
of the Nazis
marching in.

Whyever
did he then
enlarge
his progeny,
elongate them
into giant frames,
until the world
looked taller
everywhere,
and he couldn't
possibly escape
with his skinny

Garden of Eden
in any direction
from any enemy,
by any kind
of conveyance,
let alone
a bicycle . . .

Or did he
learn
that he had
to leave them
behind,
and that
was the only way
when he made
his last escape,
he would
ever
remain.

At What Point

Two months have gone by.
Some part of every day I think of them.
At what point did they know all weather
comes from the north, that the picnic
had sprouted horns, that the sea was an open
mouth and they were supper?

It is hard to plan to be swept away
by the sea, or eaten by sharks.
But at dusk the big fish come in.
At what point was it too late
to retrieve their children, the gold
they had stashed against winter,
their identity . . .
                what was their name?
                I forget. they picnicked
                at an island off the windward chain.
                never came back. no trace.

It is hard to vanish from the face of the earth.
If someone wants to find you, it is hard to vanish.
Vanity makes it hard to vanish.

            There is a point
            too late in summer, in the wind, when
            the kite fails and the birdman from Australia
            is shouting no oh no as he plummets to earth.

"Hit It with the Baby"

Rounding a corner in an open ocean
is quite possible. Landmarks,
ocean marks keep shifting but keep
coming on. That school of whales
has been here, near here before,
and our insides leap riding
the back of that great water-breaking
shape, carting his own scenery
with him. The sun careens
around the earth at a breath-taking speed
to that old hide.
                  Every dawn is a drama
played by light, surfacing surprise,
streams of color dragged across your eye
balls. That dark island which grew
in you, which you have spewed up to indent
the horizon, now has a golden hummock
to show you that it cares. No,
to show you light is all that matters
after all ("hit it with the baby," and
anyone in the theatre could walk that beam
of spot light to the stage,) and that is what
we search for, after all, not oceans,
islands, not this continual wandering about
backstage, banging our heads on the dressing room door,
but the moment on our inner stage
when we have "hit it with the baby"
            and light blooms.

Poem Found in an Old George Garrett Footprint

It is true that the wind
   is blowing in all
      secret places.

The dominoes have fallen
   stacked as a
      stairs of wheat.

Nowhere is becoming
   the chic place
      to go.

Pocahontas had a word
   for it—
      smitty, she said,

burning in all her joints,
   and hearts cracked
      open to hear—

Indians were full of
   red blood and
      necessary—

For we must lift up,
   mustn't we
      lift up?

And call, shout perhaps

    that the sun did stand
       still on a day

when the countryside came
    to town to shop
        and meander—

Oh girls in your runcible
    skins, powdered over
        with orange juice

no lazy laxen day is worth
    your hair's breadth
        gleaming with down.

Signals for Anti-Hijacking

What signals were sparking
from an antimacassar
and an 1889 sewing machine shift
where the ladies were
excited sexually. (Odd-
ment information
exchanged before
the All Aboard was repeated
sternly.) Should be on
board. You, there, behind
the rope, the barrier, the beard,
step back, stand back.
She has been cleared for flight.
Do not touch her hand.
Do not touch. Hair
oil from the city
of Macassar has threatened
every overstuffed chair
of the occident. Every pedaled
sewing machine threatened
a young girl's thighs. Crooked
seams were not the question,
angled energy was,
masturbation mechanized.
      Over each airplane headrest
high on the highbacked seats
rests the antimacassar. Anti-hijack

is the case we bandy here. Stepped
up protection for the stepped-up
threat. We look into her inmost
secrets, rifle her purse for
handgun, bomb, grenade. What
kind of electric spark is waiting
to be aroused between two poles,
the final exorcism. Here,
lady, here is your purse. Sir, you
are not allowed in here.
   An accurate scanning
would set the wings on fire,
the sirens would arouse
all Macassar. All sewing machines
would put on a burst of speed
    and head for the Celebes.

Ruminations After Saying No to Giving a College Graduation Address

My head is down here under
this pile of newspapers. I
am in hiding from
anyone who wants
guidance. The only question
I know the answer to
is 'where am I' and
I only know that
from these newspapers.

> Face the Class: You Graduates
> graduated in size and shape
> and degree of inability
> are as inadequate to meet
> the needs of the world as I was
> at your age.

>> (The professor let me read my poem
>> in full voice and confidence, then
>> opened his Shakespeare Sonnets and said
>> "Try never to write less well than this.")

When did I meet the man who
said start where you are?
(I am under these newspapers.)
I do not want to rise to headlines,
only to know where to take them
to be re-cycled. If I had had
the judgment to choose,
I would have chosen judgment.

Push

Push back the rose portieres
I am coming through.
I want my turn in the Morris Chair
with the black arm button to zing
me into orbit. Escaping always,
I am in return.

                I clutch to me
the ancient evil rights, giddy
with despair. Hopeless is a water-
fall of warning. Idiocy took off
on the morning breeze, misnamed
innocence.

                We wheeled and banked
against a calico sky, blazed
a trail (we thought) of possibles.
Oh we were birds and would grow
feathers in a minute.

                We heard
the sound of the tidal wave
and thought it was applause.

The Bagley Iowa Poem

    1.

Bagley meant to be
a railroad town
but the railroad
hadn't heard.

Three churches
poulticed
600 people.
(five ninety-nine
after I ran away.)

The sneaky holy-roller summer—
with Christian Endeavor
serving as the dating bureau—
on Main street sat the Methodist madam.

God's sparrow
never flew in our trees
and the angling birch
filling my window
turned into a creaking skeleton
when I became
homesick at home.

    2.

No was a great big
thousand letter word

and the consequences
were plenty.

Yes was love
and all that
meant, soured
and scourged
with unhappy knots
that tied the men
to their women
and the women
to their men
and the land
heaved and buckled
and produced
2¢ a bushel
    corn
and separate rooms.

3.

Bagley,
well, yes,
heaved on winter streets,
sweltered in the summer.
Grandma Plummer,
deaf as a post
hole,

traded the attic
for a double-carpeted
dining room
two husbands later.
I don't think I
was through with weddings
before I began but
the illustrations
were out of focus
and the hills
were full of accidents
and proposals.

    4.

I fly back to my childhood
trying to get the water-tower
shape right. Shaped like a—

I sneak up on it through the trees,
the apple trees that are young
and shapely. Shaped like—

There on its long spindly legs,
the fat tub of a water-tower
towers over the splattered town

shaped like a great bruise

with the welts running like
mainstreet and over it the water tower

shaped like a Roman candle
waiting to go off if only
someone would set a match to it.

I bring my torch. Water
tower shaped like Canaveral.
Over and over I have dreamed
of seeing Bagley from the moon.

    5.

Learning that the town has no more trains
                  or buses
shouldn't matter to me who will never go there
              again but
it has put me standing on a corner
under the bus stop sign
in my new graduation suit
and a hat with a flowing scarf
of a color I can't remember
but the dust is blowing—
gum wrappers mince down the street
making their small journey—
and I am headed away.

Orders

After I ran away from home and came back again,
my Papa said, Go if you must but mind three things:
stay away from water, stay off of boats, and don't
go up in an aeroplane.　　So first I learned to swim,
then I learned to sail,　 and then I learned to fly.

Separation Blues in E♭

Take the bull by his one bent horn
and look at the truth where he lies:
death for you entered when you were born,
and laughter sat in his eyes.

Death's not a valley,
death's not a hill.
We're all struck down
by our own sweet will.
With your death everyone dies.

Where is the mother who mothered me,
and where is the father who sired.
I'm grown, grown till I've mothered my own
and hell by their bones is fired.

My soul is hot where the fire seeps through
and the dreams grow fast to my feet.
Love is a woman I do not know,
a man I have yet to meet.

Air and water and land and me
and lone . . . lone . . . lone . . .
Air and water and land and sea
and bleached bent bone.

Place Counts

"Place counts," but I have brought
my prairie mind to this mountain
pasture. I observe the peaks.
Old mountains, they glow blue
as far as the eye can see, surround
my ann's laced grass, support
my flock of birds, where I am
power-mad. These are my mountains,
this is my sky. And the copperhead
under the porch is mine,
my oriental reminder that I am
full of fear and ancientness
that all the analysis in the world
can only label or identify.

Great breathing heaving meadow
that incites my prairie mind
to joy, if place cannot be sky,
      I choose you.

In Retrospect

This is my house, I can pace the floor,
shut out a mouse, unlock a door,
sit on the stair and look up and down.
    Why are the flowers turning brown?
The stair of my youth was a closed-in stair.
I had to sit for punishment there.
(To suffocate, parsed on the middle tread.)
    Why are the flower faces dead?

Hung on the wall was a brown bouquet,
the bouquet of flowers she picked that day.
Once they were fresh as her own cheek's bloom.
I cannot breathe in this box-like room.
Hydrangea rages around my head,
everything living is suddenly dead,
with a picture to prove it, a coffin scene,
for the three year old (when I reached sixteen)
    and a gift of flowers, dead and gone,
        hung like geese with their feathers down.
            (In her closed-in tomb has she withered brown?)

I should have done, I should have done
follows me everywhere I've gone.
I should have taken the flowers down.
    What good's a bouquet with the flowers brown?
I should have thrown what they tried to save
in the open mouth of my mother's grave.

Conjure Blues

Guilty, once, of driving the cat
madder than maggots, with catnip
never intended for anything more
than summoning luck on a ship,
        bringing them safely home.

The cat Vincent (for Price)
Bartholomew, for Saint and Church,
ran in angled circles,
recognizing dervishes,
        bringing them safely home.

Now if the dog leaps at the Nairn
games at tossing the caber
and the bagpipes whinny a tune
they learned from the wind,
while mid-summer boys
bleat carols on an air of snow,
then we will know real witches are
        bringing you safely home.

Nightshade Family

I run through the meadow spilling poems
I can't afford to lose. I am looking
for snakes and thistles and poison-
        ous ground cherries.

I want to write about forgiving
my enemy. But I haven't forgiven
her. Poetry is fiction they told me
        once. Nonsense.

Everything beneath her has rotted
away. Nothing is left of the house
where she used to live. But she still sits
        on the porch and rocks.

She chases me through the meadow in
her rocking chair. It travels faster
than most horses I know. It travels faster
        than swans.

I think of feeding her poisonous cherries
but she would take nothing to eat from me.
The last supper I fed her was of crooked neck
        yellow squash

which she had left as a present on my porch
while she was still my friend. Now the poison meant
for the thistles is killing the trees, and my hands
        are on her yellow crooked neck.

A Measure Of Hate

When you are considering incomprehensible amounts,
think of rain.

Down the mountainside behind my lodge came a river
big as the Missouri.

It was gone when the sun came out. I went outside
to film the waterfall.

There was only a trickle of water bumping down
the shining stone

so small that at some angles, it was camouflaged.
So much for waterfalls.

But when the rain began again so did that water slide,
and I was multiplying

in my mind all the nearby mountains in the Lake Country,
in Snowdonia,

in all the rest of Wales, down the ribbed coast, over
"Paddy's Puddle"

all the Irish mountains, Iceland, Greenland, Newfoundland, everywhere it was raining,

waterfalls were pouring themselves down mountain slides
that my film

would never solidify. Water will be re-cycled
from some ocean.

The sun will drink the lake. But it is the number
of water drops

I ask you to consider. Taken one by one it could take
the rest of your life.

So much for the rest of your life.

Every Now and Then at Night

Every now and then at night
when a billowed cloud this side the moon
rides black and madam-like, I think of her.

Standing against the velvet draperies
in the almost pitch-dark room, she
was the only shining thing.

Bulbous woman who peddled booze
in a dry county in a checkerboard wet dry state
in a wet war country, and all

that rot-gut she sold us
should have been pure silver
for the price we paid.

And we drank ourselves to lunacy
on our one night off the base.
We knew nobody but ourselves for a thousand miles.

So we dreamed she
was our black and shining mother,
and she was.

Lines Written While Landing at La Guardia

I am
spiraling
in over North
Brother Island
squinting for
Typhoid Mary's
hut, close to the
lighthouse on
the corner toward
South Brother
where those stranded
sailors spent the night
trying to attract a rescue
and drive off rats
with their scrubby fire.

I hear
the spiraling
heat coming on
through the clanking pipes
in the Nurses' Quarters
partitioned into
living quarters
for such as us,
the veterans. Pay
the rent to Mr. Pink
and try to have a baby
to zoom down-river
by police-boat
to Bellevue's
obstetrics

ward.
But
it was too soon.
A one-year baby
lived with us
and laid her
head
on her coconut
cake because
it was shaped
like a lamb.

I hear
the drunken
ferry captain
glancing the ship
from side to side
in the ferry slip
with every docking.
He rolled
the same old ferry
right on to Rikers
on visiting days
for the prisoners.
We were all
prisoners trying
to love
something,
trying to
attract
a rescue.

Gussie Sends Quick Letter

Dear Orlando, Sometimes I remember
when you tried to send me one rose
just after the geranium gas and the one
that smelled like cucumber
when we inched our way into that old house
and quick took off our gas masks
and quick put them back on
so we would know if we smelled anything funny
just what we were dying of,
                              and I guess
if you'd ordered a funeral wreath
or a bushel of cucumbers they would have
sent them but one rose they said no to
and that was the end of us. Love, Gussie.

The Witch of Calmés

Now when the vision comes down from the mountain
and clangs at the door of my grave
country house, (haven't you replaced her yet?)
what kind of pirouette is this we play?
You fill, I back, I fill, you back away,
flaying as you go. This was no dance
ever taught to me. I stiffen in a chairlike
stance, and sit upon myself. Deliberate.

    Now you come moving in from the mountain.
(Can I believe you snuggled there alone?)
You move slow-motion, taking giant steps,
made possible by the parachute winded on your back,
skull-faced—like Golding's ghost—making for the sea,
but you are trodding bodies, facing me.
And I fall back upon my witch upbringing,
that the dervish is a lonesome whirl,
and you, wind-motored, are wind only
and I have shed my skin, my skin of girl.

    Since witches do not weep, all this water
is merely ash from burnt-out lies
that rivers through the wrinkles,
spraying from my cheeks,
making catlike whiskers, great bow-ties.

Tradition hardens, turning envious eyes
to bitter green and glowing. I too
move to the mountain in slow-motion.
    I will lift alone toward canceled skies.

Looking for Origins

Here on the mountain the thistles
are riding their purple swath.
They translate into dollar signs
in town, prickly all the way.

If I could sell bread, I mean
a loaf I punched and muttered into,
and put in the right-temperatured oven,
I might survive and pay the rent,

but translation is always here.
Something into something else.
I keep thinking maybe a color will
survive, or a tune on a hollow reed.

I should know better.
Survival is for the fittest.
But I remember a man
who knew where he started. And told us

to start where we were. Someday I might
be able to do what he said.
He had conquered his thistles, his
purple. The loaf was in his head.

Country Tract

Whenever you are wined
your thumbs come hard
before anything else does.
I shout in the night
trying to reach you
in your log of wine-bark.

Sex is rarer in town
than the cercoleptes
caudivolvulus. There
dancing naked is frowned
upon and shouts in the night
are investigated.

We clutch our wilderness
cover conversation with
wildflowers, but
it is our wild
that flowers here.

Homing

All those poems that got away
last night are fluttering
up—white moths

and I have returned to my cage
on the top of the world
to find the lilies have stalked
and bloomed and I am a fraud:

in this bitter world
I am consumed with joy.

Distance

All my life I have watched you coming up the hill,
past the hanging tree, the barbed-wire bull,
and as you pass, I wave from my window.

> this is the window where the woman
> is always shading her eyes from the sun,
> watching the distance come closer,
> enclose her. Glaucoma.

I know you better than the back of my hand.
I was never given to studying the back
of my hand. Palm, yes, I read the palm
and watch it dissolve in the dish water.

> this is the window which the snow reached.
> the woman sitting alone in the blizzard,
> her man walking twenty miles from town,
> she put a candle in the window to keep her company
> and that's how he learned he'd been walking
> in circles for hours. One frozen foot.

I still see you walking up the hill. Is it only
one trip you have made? why is there no house
around this window? I carry this frame.

The Case of the
Red Dotted Swiss

When I remember us, we
are in a picture,
I am two feet high
and the hand I'm holding
is still attached to
my palm.
      The picture
is full of gifts, the light,
the golden curls, the red
dotted swiss dress that hangs
all the way to the grass.

I am barefooted, I feel
the earth under my feet the way
I feel that hand under my hand.
Laughter floats all around us.
I can smell the meadow grass,
the sweet smell of the orchard.
I can hear his voice if I listen.
I can feel sun through red dotted swiss.

Death Watch

Again it is ten-thirty in the morning,
it is nine-thirty where you are.
Death is at eleven o'clock, coming
in fast. You have shot back
all of your ammunition.

What you feared most, you said,
was coming to the end the way she did,
the shriveled woman
whom you fed through a false
opening. Now all your openings are
cemented shut. You fed us misery
through line after line
of your cemented letters.
They made us want to keep
the distance at least as far
as when we ran away.

It is ten forty-five in the morning,
it is nine-forty-five where you are.
The distance is always the same.
What curse do I fear if
I do not care enough.
I have forgiven you your hate.

What really happened when
our mother died? How

did the feud start? Was it true,
about the coat and cap of fur,
were they yanked off me?
Did someone plan
an orphanage for you?
These stories fed to me through false
openings, were meant to cement me
to one feuding side. How could I
have known I was the ammunition.

It is eleven o'clock in the morning,
it is ten o'clock where you are.
The distance is cemented.
I am counting my ammunition.

It is twelve o'clock.

The Trip

                The tent
was new and smelled of creosote.
We were fairly new ourselves
and smelled of joy and ambition.

When the storm came up we hardly
knew it was coming. The sky
turned wondrous green and we
admired it momentarily until
we remembered it wasn't
a color for skies.

The tent blew away very quickly
and the little boat pitched
and wavered on the fast chop lake
that looked as if it had never
practiced waves before.
                They came
from every direction, and we
hardly knew what to cling to.
When it was over that's all we knew.

Two Men
in Tractor Time

1.

He
     approaches Allis as if this iron maiden
     had leapt full grown from the Chalmers tractor factory.
     As if so 'twere, 'twould go, crunch air,
           and Allis does!
     Strains ancient joints, flakes rust demurely down,
     clears her oiled throat, leaps door jamb
     in gay abandon, ready to outstrip her guarantee,
     long lost in sales from second hand to hand.
     Allis moves as if she'd just
     graduated from tractor dancing class,
     whisks bobbetting over the pasture grass,
     nipping the eager thistling pods, the filament
     balloons of seed-head, dead-head dandelions,
     and the aromatic clover licking the breeze.
          Ah, Allis, Wonder-maid!

2.

He
     approaches Allis as if this goon had crept
     half-finished from the tractor factory . . . as if
     the wheel were a yet-to-be-discovered thing.
     As if the tractor were made of stone, to be
     hewed again each time its strength was needed.
     As if the mesh of gears had been, by proclamation,

solidified. And if some foreign magic makes her start,
choke, smoking bilious clouds of gas and oil,
changing the sunny landscape to a darkening fog,
then Allis charges like a young bull elephant,
every stick tickling its unders. Enraged,
she carves the hill with streaked ruts,
and, magnetized by the life-sized trees,
flips her rider off on a jutted curve
and heads for imminent collision.
      Allis, Queen of Diminishment!

To a Father Stewing About His Sons

Old man, old man, you cannot taste
        the soup in all the kettles,
nor salt nor ladle each.
Do not despair that they are out of reach.
Their tongues will tell them.
Trust in their taste.

        Born of you
        thorn to you
        thrown from you

the seasoning not done in haste,
the finished feast is theirs to waste
or savor.   Stir yourself.

Bone-China Woman

That Bone-China woman with the Geiger-counter eye
    has tapped my guilt mine, suctioned in
    with hospitals for cripples, mangled
    children, elderly stricken, mental
    tragedies, blind. She can diagram
    pity out of its purposelessness.

I being blind, and crippled,
    often mentally deranged,
    too old for youth rates,
    childish in my preference,
    am afraid of her.

She will have me tap-tapping my neighbor's door
    who will be glad to see me, if surprised,
    until she sees I carry those small cards.

    If I see Bone-China coming up my walk,
    I'll dive into my tincup and drown.

History Has Struck Her Repeat Button

That three-knobbed elbow that you rocked
me with, soft as a clover in my recollection,
has rounded the corner of my shoulder
and now appears on my left arm. I didn't
fall from that see-saw. You did. and wracked
your arm into a singular structure
that swayed my lullaby nights. Now this:
I've wished it onto myself. I wanted
your wrinkles and your soft skin,
even the corns from your dancing feet.
They are mine. Complete with
an arm that anchors me three knobbed
to three wishes. that I grow old, old, old.

Note to the Young Girl
Who Has Just Won a Poetry Prize

Child, your compliment congeals
my coursing liquid gauge of what
is coming and going in my center
of the world.
                You said:
now maybe I can be like you,
and I wanted to tell you no, no,
don't follow me through this thicket.
There's too much aching
in the woods already, don't
generate another crippled view
of the possibilities. Live
at a full stretch, don't
follow me down here under
this stone. Find yourself
a meadow of wild flowers,
or set up a small store—
antiques or toys—or even
books if you have to stay
that close to words, but when
you sell your soul to the poems
you'll learn there is a Lucifer,
a fact you didn't have to know.
Praise God, in case, the poet said,
but paid the Devil anyway.
That's the way it is.
Once you've developed

the double vision, there he sits
on the fence post, cracking your bones
in his teeth and spitting out the sinews.
Stay where the sun makes shadows
you can identify, not this—not
this shaking that makes you
ask me if I'm cold.

The Animal Standing There

1.

The lady or the poet. If
I walk on a stage
dedicated to Shakespeare by
a dedicated man named Folger,
I will wear velvet and a pleated
ruff with blue satin ribbon.
If that is a jeweled mask,
so be it. If the poems turn
out to be rigged for stoning,
so be that too. It will be
no worse than lying down to sleep
driven by the sling of stones,
to rise each morning with
the bruised and battered news,
the day. What animal is this?
the poet or the lady.

2.

When my children were through
with the sandbox we had built
I took it apart, bagged sand
and drove twenty miles to find
a place where I could dump it
legally. The boards were carved

with termites, and they scurried—
white-bellied eaters—behind my closed
lids when I tried to sleep at night.
and they chewed and spittled, and St
Mark's mosaics were being removed
piece by delicate piece because
the termites chewed and spittled.
Venice may be sinking into the sea,
or the sea could be rising to shroud
that queen of cities. Sin could shake
St Marks in its foundation,
but if the termites lay the cathedral
low, what animal will be left
standing.

3.

I have been doing a striptease
since the day of the wishing game:
If you could be anybody you wanted to—
and I said Sarah Bernhardt and they said
we thought you'd have picked
Florence Nightingale.

The more my outer clothes come off
the more my skin turns alligator.
Some briny morning the outside
will meet the inside and the animal
standing there will be a stranger.

*Late Last Night
with Southern Comfort*

Sail bonny billy goat,
bird of prayer, hawking
wares of beginnings again,
hush be thy name near the old gum tree.
Hist where the fashion of gallantry brought us.
Love is the word leaking treasure for me.
Love must be the word, or the measure of leaving
is broiled in an oil that is grizzly, unpure,
(and hate is as common as taxing is sure.)
Hangdog conundrums are sailing with sunset,
night is a bellyache charged with starfire.
(Strange widows peer in at the door.)
Upset at moonset, the briefs are polluted,
the concerts are over, the music has fled.
Haste, hurry, the bloated beginnings are over,
the knife is half buried, the currents are dead.
Sweet was a word that was married with meaning
till silence ensued through the holes in the head.

November Park

There are no children in the park
There is an old man who dribbles
There is a young mother who thinks
I am an old woman in a void.

All the children who sailed skyward
in these swings have sailed away
All the mothers have withered
on their bones, have wrinkled
their promises to fit the altitude.

(On this same bench she sat
until the snow covered her,
first her tracks, then the folds
between her fingers. Filled
with pills she sat so still.)

I sit and wait for the young mother
to quietly fold the park
place it in her handbag
and saunter skyward.

To Write

Must you be mad to write?
Out of touch with meanings that preserve your skin?
Soaring blindly with no map back, lost
even to yourself?
especially to yourself?

If this is the entry
price, the cost of lying flat on pages
till the books are burnt,
only a fool would buy a ticket.

But they were giving passes away
the day I came upon words,
and oh my god the sound
was what my ache was named.

Until Cremation Is Required

You have arrived in a small box not large enough
to contain your head.

Your smile cannot curve these ashes, the loss is
circumferential.

When I have reached your eighty odd, if I do,
I may change my mind.

I do not think I will change it to ashes.
For too many years

I was threatened by hell-fire for my gross
sins of thought, of wish.

Yearned too often for too many, was sentenced
to be burned alive.

I looked on sights I was not supposed to see,
listened while the bones

talked. They are sacred. How dare the scholars burn
your bones. Your skull

could have smiled for centuries. Could have made
a home for a shrew. Or the Oracle of Ge.

The Formula

When I start to write
the formula for living
on the board, it's not
that the chalk crumbles,
but that my hand
disappears.

Yorick Rides Again

I

Dreaming in color
I have come
by some map
to the steps
of this old house.

If I go in the door,
it will bang shut
and I can never
get out again.

      Is this anticipating?
rolling the stone to the mouth of the cave?
only one way to practice this: roll
the stone to the mouth of someone else's death.
      Are we all murderers?
Must I put this together with plurals?
is the singular too singular, too jugular,
to produce, inside, the necessary weight
to push back on the pressure per square inch?

      Just remember to remember.
      Face it straight. no lies.
      no scalloped explanation.
      That's the only way

  it is all bearable.
  The eyelash glue
  will glue your eyelids shut.
  Go bald if need be.
  There is YES and KNOW.

There's a crazy old lady with a thorn in her paw.
Mount that and ride it away.
And the writer of the horoscope said
this was the day to come upon my love
and there is nobody here but me.
Recover from that as slowly as you like.
Or go back. do I dare go back?

   Suddenly there is an egg on my desk,
   a sworled stone egg. The past
     is as easy to crack.

     II

My dream begins with head in hand
and the flesh changes under my wish.
Is this my civilized way to handle
murder? I have wished women dead
and they have died. Guilt hangs
on my neck like a sloth.

"A man comes true as I think him"
Shall I conjure my dead love? Be made
love to by a shade? "You've a chance
to be more," he said, his red hair
gleaming through dappled light.
I loved his angularity, the way his bones
bent, the feel of his skin.

>Dare as much as you're able.
>Set your mark upon some tree
>or other. Make one of the rings
>to be counted, yours.

>I dreamed of being Clara Bow.
>(Never heard of her.) made
>calling cards on my printing
>press. Enchanted names,
>Douglas Fairbanks, Mary
>Pickford, Lon Chaney,
>names vibrate me into song.

And there we sat in the Captain's Chair
in the back of the movie house,
me on my Papa's lap. And we watched
the whole BIG PARADE go by. Followed
by CIMARRON, and all the daring

derring-do, and I was as brave
as sitting on the Captain's lap
could make me. We were in Charge.
And that is as close as we ever came.

>   I have broken the stream ice in order
>   to paddle the canoe into the fast flowing
>   river to reach the mountain point by water.
>   I had overcome the fear . . . no,
>   I did it anyway.

>   I have spent the first half of my life
>   overcoming my fear of water. Shall
>   I spend the last half overcoming my fear
>   of earth?

>   III

Yorick rocks in my house like rhyme.
Yorick sways back and forth in the wind.
Our riddle Yorick with his long brown feet . . .
                    But look!
in the hands of an artist, the quick
business of the suddenly opened jaw.
Shakespeare, come back for a minute,
come look upon your clown: ". . . but age,

with his stealing steps,
hath claw'd me in his clutch . . ."
                        Flash open
the skull into a leering grin
the closer I come to the form,
the more I know that even this is holy.
And the bone forms or melts with the words,
even the words revolving in my skull
lapping like prisoned birds (are these
the forms I see in my side vision?)

        All I wanted was not to be laughed at.
        ("It ain't no sin to take off your skin
           and dance around in your bones.")
        unless I meant to be
        funny.

        I was safe as long as I
        remembered exactly what I said
        to everyone. Now they tell me
        he was in love with me,
        and I cannot even find
        the place on the porch
        where the air closed around him.

        Could it be? that for every

young man I have loved,
someone loved me?

>Oh the rules that keep us woven together
>into patterns of the wrong color. Rules
>that if broken go snapping in the wind
>beating us with their fractured ends
>until we develop a thickening so we
>no longer feel anything.

IV

We sat in church
he scalded by my red dress
and opened the only hymnal there
in Memoriam to my mother.
He never went to church again,
not even in his coffin.

They say that before his funeral
before the preacher arrived, someone
went out and sawed the dead limb
off the old cedar. I keep wondering
whether it was Papa
>or me.

Did I think as long as I didn't see him dead
he wouldn't be? Hold me
on your lap again and tell me
a funny story. Horty, make me laugh.

I am coming to this half-way point
unloved by anyone but you. The word goes
flopping about and I want to say hush, hush
don't waste the word. We are needy.
Love is All is love is

V

I am up one step of this sagging porch
of this gaunt house, riddled by rage and incongruities.
Put it together like a puzzle. (Is that their claim?
into the three A M with little convoluted pieces of
colored cardboard, putting myself together?
thinking if I put the edges together first, my edges
will resolve?) Oh pickled desire on the shelf turning
moldy, damn damn damn

Puzzles are not enough. I want the wind to turn
warm suddenly, in the hot blaze of
seeing you coming down the street,

your coat flowing, and we are suddenly
enmeshed in winter wool and
each others arms. To hell with the apostrophe.
and is this what they call maturing?
this next broken step?

        I had hoped there would be Point Wise.
        I had hoped the middle would
        suddenly blaze with TRUTH!
        There is only this old house
        with the broken steps, leading to
        the fractured porch, and inside, inside . . .
        my god, I must open the door.

      Why didn't one of you tell me,
      one of you who said you loved me,
      that the only rules that counted
      were the ones I invented
      as I went along.

They Asked Me What I Wanted

All I wanted was
Grandfather's bell.

They asked me what I wanted.
I said: Grandfather's bell.

How many years ago did I say:
all I want is Grandfather's bell.

A farm bell. A bell that rang
for breakfast, dinner, supper,

emergency. No one uses
Grandfather's bell.

Stored in a basement, wrapped
in rags. No one rings it.

Everyone left the farm, stored
Grandfather's bell.

We have no farm. Twenty-one acres
is no farm. But the bell

could ring, I'd ring it.
I would listen.

Why can't I have
Grandfather's bell?

Because I want it.

I don't know
any way to hurry it.